hiSTORY OF iRELAND

history of ireland

This is a Tara Book
This edition published in 2000
Tara is an imprint of Parragon

Parragon
Queen Street House
4 Queen Street
Bath BA1 1HE, UK

Produced by Magpie Books, an imprint of
Constable & Robinson Ltd, London

By Harry Adès

Designed by Tony and Penny Mills

ISBN 1-902879-11-2

A copy of the British Library Cataloguing-in-Publication Data is available
from the British Library

Printed and bound in China

ACKNOWLEDGEMENTS

The picture on p21 is reproduced by permission of The British Library;
those on pp11 and 12 are by courtesy of the National Museum of Ireland;
pp36–7 and pp40–1 of the National Gallery of Ireland; pp52 and 57 The
Mary Evans Picture Library. The picture on the jacket and that on p47 is
by the marine artist Rodney Charman, whose work is exhibited here and in
the USA. We are very grateful for his permission to reproduce it here. It
appears by courtesy of the Egan Foundation, Nantucket, USA. The picture
on p52 is by kind permission of the Central Bank of Ireland

CONTENTS

introduction

Glorious and painful, hopeful and desperate, joyful and tragic, Ireland's history arouses the emotions like no other. It is a history that spans the spectrum of human experience, of an island that led the world in art and cultivation, that was buffeted and battered by conquest and invasion, that was torn apart by religion, resettlement and partition, that was devastated by famine and war, and that came at last to the threshold of peace.

The brief history in this book attempts to capture the defining moments, from the most obscure beginnings of prehistory to the groundbreaking events of the present day, that have formed a nation and its people.

ORIGINS OF A NATION

The human history of Ireland begins nine thousand years ago. For the earliest inhabitants, life on the island was spent hunting and fishing. Little is known for sure, but some say they navigated the rivers and seas on tiny skin coracles scouring the chilly waters for fish. Others claim that they wandered about the country's lush pine, elm and oak forests clutching simple flint weapons, in pursuit of Irish Elk, giant deer standing six feet at the shoulder with antlers spanning eight feet like monstrous hands of bone.

By about 3000 BC, a farming people tilled the good land and reared animals. They made strong axes from polished stone, they spun and wove

cloth, they moulded pots and tools of clay and they built houses of wood and thatch. They also made great monuments for their dead and for their gods. Thousands of these dot the Irish countryside, silent testaments of a lost civilization: lonely standing stones five metres high, dolmens of great boulders balanced on top of legs of rock, stones set in careful circles and straight lines. Most impressive of all were their tombs, the passage graves built with huge stone slabs weighing many tons, covered under a mound of earth.

Newgrange, on the River Boyne near Drogheda, is the finest surviving example of a Neolithic tomb, and one of the most important prehistoric sites in the world. A slender twenty-metre passageway leads from outside into the heart of the tomb. On winter solstice sunrise, sunlight beams down the passageway, bathing the tomb inside with a wintry glow. There can be no doubt that these were knowledgeable and organized people, sophisticated architects and experts in the movements of the sun and stars.

The entrance to Newgrange

This culture was on the wane in the second millennium BC. The metalworkers of Bronze Age Ireland hammered out countless tools and weapons, so many that they could export their products to Britain in large numbers. Eventually the craftsmen found a new medium for their work. Gold from the rivers of the Wicklow mountains was made into exquisite jewellery, dazzling gold collars, torcs and gorgets to be worn by society's most important people. The prehistoric land of gold, Ireland's goldsmiths crafted more precious pieces than anywhere else in Europe.

At around 500 BC evidence exists of unrest and upheaval. Fortifications were built against waves of fierce invaders. They came from the east, from central Europe, warriors brandishing new and deadly weapons, swords of iron and hard-tipped spears. Their superior armaments, larger stature and their horse-drawn chariots made them more than a match for the bronze-working defenders. These warlike people were the Celts, who over the centuries were to shape Ireland more than any other culture, giving future generations an art, religion, a language and a way of life.

There are no written records of early Irish Celtic society. Laws, customs, history and religion were all passed on by word of mouth. The *fili*, wandering poets and bards, committed to memory all sorts of rules, rituals, stories and news through rhythm and verse. They enjoyed the highest social standing along with other *aes dána* ('people of skill'), such as the druids, smiths, artists and musicians.

The Celts did not build towns and cities, so had no need for roads. Kings and chieftains ruled over their tribes within small territories or *tuatha*. Incessant fighting and cattle-raiding made them worry far more about the neighbouring tribe than an invasion from over the seas. The Roman historian Tacitus tells us that Agricola dearly wanted to take Ireland. But on the farthest reaches of the known world, this lonely, windswept island, home of the fierce and belligerent Celts, was never invaded by the Romans.

In fact, the next 'invasion' of Ireland was cultural rather than military. It was to pave the way for a golden age in Irish history, when the country led the world in artistic expression and virtuosity. Christianity came gently to Ireland over many years, perhaps spread by the word of missionaries, traders, travellers and refugees from the collapsing Roman Empire. By 431 there were enough Christians in the south of the country for Pope Celestine to give Ireland her first bishop, Palladius.

It is St Patrick, however, who is traditionally credited for converting the Irish. He was born of a Romano-British family near Carlisle. When he was a boy, raiders from Ulster captured him and threw him into slavery. He worked for six years as a shepherd, before escaping to Gaul. In 432 he returned, driven by an unquenchable desire to preach the teachings of Christ to his pagan captors. Patrick must have had a gift for persuasion; he sowed the seeds of Christianity through the established Celtic ways, and it blossomed without the sprinkling of a single

martyr's blood. The kings, *fili* and druids gave way to him easily, adapting their sacred sites according to Christian needs.

Christianity was so well established by the beginning of the sixth century that monasteries were being built across the country, due to the great zeal of the early founders. Such was the devotion of St Brendan of Clonfert, for example, that he sailed the seas in a coracle as far as the Canary Islands to spread the word of God.

The isolated farms and villages of the Celtic system were ideally suited to monastic life, and the monasteries flourished. They became great

centres of learning, cradles of art and literature, havens to craftsmen, metalworkers and calligraphers, fleeing the barbarian hordes that swept across the continent in the wake of Rome's demise. In these cultivated sanctuaries Christianity opened the way to a new artistic expression, one that the Irish seized with alacrity, spurred on by a new range of styles and techniques that complemented the Celtic traditions perfectly.

The new religion supplanted the old pagan world, introducing new signs and symbols onto the old sacred objects. The tall standing stones, venerated since prehistory, evolved into Ireland's famous stone high crosses. Decorating the grounds of monasteries across the country, the crosses (many still stand) towered up to twenty feet in height, each face and shaft elegantly carved with biblical stories, holy saints and scenes from Christ's life.

For the metalworkers the unifying belief in a single God also gave a new focus for their craft. The torcs and gorgets of pagan times were replaced with glittering objects of Christian worship. Churches filled with gleaming artefacts, brilliant shrines and wrought crosses, croziers, book-covers and chalices. The spectacular Ardagh Chalice, found in 1868 by a young boy as he dug up a potato field in County Limerick, is of such breathtaking quality that the intricate filigree work has been hailed the finest of any age.

The priests would have worn glittering penannular brooches, an ornament that had been popular long before the eighth century, when the most sublime example was created. The Tara Brooch was discovered in a wooden box on the mouth of the Boyne in County Meath. It was named after the legendary royal seat of Ireland, as it was truly thought to be worthy of high kings and queens. Employing every known technique of the age, the brooch embodies the pinnacle of early Irish metalwork.

Even the written word, which the Celts had long reviled as damaging to memory and the power of thought, achieved new heights that some say have never since been equalled. Among several surviving illuminated manuscripts of the

The Ardagh Chalice

The Tara Brooch (reverse)

time, the *Book of Kells* is widely regarded to be the most extraordinary. The origins of the book are obscure, but most agree that it was started in a monastery founded by St Columba in the sixth century on the Scottish island of Iona. He was a keen scribe and made sure that his monks followed the practice of writing and copying the holy scriptures. By the time they embarked upon the *Book of Kells* in the early eighth century, his monks were masters of calligraphy, and commanded a dazzling array of styles and techniques to entrance the reader.

Nowhere else is found such minute and perfect knotwork, interweaving ribbons, writhing and wrestling animals, solemn portraits, such fanciful imagery all painted in such lustrous colours. The blazing blue *lapis lazuli* was brought in tiny quantities and at great expense from a faraway mine in Afghanistan.

The story of the manuscript's survival is almost as miraculous as its contents. By the end of the eighth century, the Vikings were raiding the islands and coasts of Scotland and Ireland. The monasteries, so full of riches, were obvious

Q

R

Q

ET

Ad [tendite]

AD

AI

AT i[lli]

14

targets. In 805 the Vikings came to Iona in their longboats. Pagans with no understanding of the sanctity of the Church, they slaughtered dozens of monks and stripped the place of its holy objects, melting them down into coins. Luckily, the magnificent manuscript was saved and spirited away to the monastery at Kells where work continued.

The coming of the Vikings, however, spelt the end of Ireland's golden age, and marked the beginning of centuries of turmoil and bloodshed at the hands of overseas powers. Yet the artistic achievements of this period remain lasting symbols of Irish nationhood.

(Opposite) Initials from The Book of Kells

invasions, conquests and rebellions

Throughout the ninth century the Viking attacks became more consistent and systematic, and met with little resistance. The 150 Irish kings and chieftains were so busy fighting among themselves that the Vikings easily overpowered them. By the end of the first millennium the Vikings had control of all but the north of the country, and had established important settlements that would become great cities of Ireland: Dublin, Cork, Limerick, Wexford, Waterford and Wicklow.

It took one of Ireland's great early leaders, Brian Boru, a fine and cunning warrior, to unite

the country. A Munster prince, Brian swiftly rose to power and proclaimed himself as High King of Ireland by 1002. Only the rebellious Leinstermen resisted him, joining forces with the Vikings to try to oust him. They met for battle at Clontarf on Good Friday 1014. Brian's army won a resounding victory, but he, by now an old man, was foolishly left alone in a tent a little away from the fighting. A fleeing Norseman saw he was unguarded and slew him.

Brian had done much good for Ireland. A devoted Christian, he set about the rebuilding of the monasteries and the restoration of the libraries. He had pacified and helped convert the Vikings, who now lived with the Irish in harmony. He showed how a united country was far stronger than a divided one. His example, sadly, was not heeded for very long. Shortly after his death, Ireland once again descended into the darkness of internal battling between the four provinces, Munster, Leinster, Ulster and Connacht, for the High Kingship. As they had done centuries earlier with the Vikings, the warring kings left the door wide open for the next invaders.

The death of Brian Boru

The highly-trained, castle-building Anglo-Norman forces came in 1169, invited by one of these kings, Dermot MacMurrough of Leinster, and authorized by Papal decree. Brave as they were, striding into battle in linen shirts with simple axes, the Irish could not prevent the armour-clad Normans from advancing deep into the country. By 1250 the invaders controlled all but the least hospitable lands to the far west and north.

For nearly two centuries, the Norman kings of England extracted taxes, supplies and soldiers from Ireland to wage other wars, notably against the Scots and Welsh. But as resources flooded out of the country, Ireland herself was being dangerously neglected. An invasion by the Scots in 1315 exposed all the weaknesses of the Anglo-Norman colonization. The incursion was eventually quelled, (and their leader's head sent to Edward II in London as a trophy) but the Norman grip never properly recovered.

The Scottish attacks had laid to waste huge tracts of land; towns lay in ruins, harvests failed and numerous estates were abandoned. Nor could the English crown rely on the colonists that stayed. The barons and noble families that should have taken up arms against the invaders by now felt far closer to the Irish than the English; they had married Irish women and taken the Irish language and customs. The infamous Statutes of Kilkenny drafted in 1366 were an attempt to prevent the further mixture and dilution of English culture. They could never be properly enforced and were largely ignored.

Gaelic power was surging, more so since the native Irish kings had learnt a new mode of battle from the Scottish 'gallowglasses' (meaning 'foreign troops'), well-drilled mercenaries who wore steel helmets and chain mail coats. The situation was so bad for the English that Richard II made two expeditions to Ireland at the end of the fourteenth century. He achieved little and in his absence ended up losing the throne too. By 1450 the English crown held sway only over the government seat at Dublin and the so-called English Pale, a sliver of land around the city thirty-miles long and twenty-miles wide. The control of Ireland fell to the Anglo-Norman lords, in particular, the Fitzgeralds of Kildare, who became the kings of Ireland in all but name.

As the English royals battled with the French in the Hundred Years' War and between themselves in the War of the Roses, Ireland was sidelined. Not until 1534 did Henry VIII take interest in the colony again, when he effectively ended the Kildare supremacy by killing the heir, 'Silken' Thomas, and putting his five uncles to the sword for good measure. He imposed English law and customs, taking land from both the Gaelic and Anglo-Irish lords and regranting it under English-style earldoms. In 1541 a special parliament officially declared Henry the King of Ireland.

Yet the English position was still precariously weak outside the Pale, and by the time Elizabeth became Queen, Ireland seemed quite a liability to English national security. As a Protestant monarch, Elizabeth feared alliances between Ireland and Catholic France or Spain, and possible invasion. Her attempts to foist Protestantism on Ireland

(Overleaf) The Irish King of Leinster rides out from the woods to meet Richard II's envoy, the Earl of Gloucester.

through colonization were largely fruitless, and growing tension between the countries led to four rebellions.

Hugh O'Neill, the Earl of Tyrone, led the most successful challenge to English authority, defeating the Queen's Deputy at the Battle of the Yellow Ford in 1598. Elizabeth sent the Earl of Essex with twenty thousand men to quash the rebels. He was an able soldier but played straight into O'Neill's hands by being drawn into a series of small skirmishes rather than one great battle. In a couple of months his army had been whittled down to only four thousand and Elizabeth's vision of a crushing victory had evaporated. Essex was summoned back to London and executed for his failure.

King Philip III of Spain weighed into the fray, sending almost five thousand troops to help O'Neill, but they landed in Kinsale, County Cork, and not Ulster where they were most needed. O'Neill had to march the length of the country before he could plan his next move, and by then the Queen's forces had regrouped under the new commander, Mountjoy. At Kinsale on Christmas Eve 1601, the armies clashed, and

The Earl of Essex

25

The flight of the Earl of Tyrone

Mountjoy's men proved too much for the combined Irish and Spanish forces.

O'Neill's life was spared by the new king, James I – a martyr was the last thing he wanted to stir the Gaels to another revolt. But O'Neill lived in fear and, although he was restored as Earl of Tyrone, had no desire to stay under English rule. He and 98 Gaelic aristocrats left the country in 1607, never to return. James quickly declared them traitors and seized their lands. The 'Flight of the Earls' was a double disaster for Ireland. It marked the end of the old Gaelic order, and allowed James to embark on the Plantation of Ulster, laying the firm foundations of religious strife that the province has suffered ever since.

protestants and catholics

The Plantation of Ulster started apace. The province was drawn into plots of a thousand acres which were handed to incoming Protestant settlers from England and Scotland. They were supposed to remove all Irish natives from their lands, but the Irish made good tenants, having to pay triple rents to the English crown. Instead of being wholly Protestant, then, Ulster became a province divided, the victim of a three-way rupture that proved most resistant to repair: landowners against the dispossessed, Protestants against Catholics, and English or Scottish against the Irish. Such was its 'success' that other plantations were launched across Ireland.

When Charles I came to the throne in 1625 it was hoped that he would show more tolerance to the Catholic population. After all, his wife was a Catholic. However, it was his dwindling finances rather than religious justice that concerned him and he set about trying to extract as much revenue from Ireland as he could. The huge influx of settlers, many of them skilled craftsmen or farmers, had stimulated productivity enormously, and he wanted to milk as much money from the island as he could. Thomas Wentworth, later the Earl of Strafford, was the man chosen for the job.

He rigorously went about his task, extracting fines and revenues from Protestants as well as Catholics, from Gaels, 'Old English' (the established Anglo-Norman gentry, who were also Catholics) and new settlers alike. He managed to collect huge sums of money, making enemies in all sections of the population as he went. 'Black Tom Tyrant' became so unpopular that when impeached in 1640 by an English parliament increasingly hostile to the King, a large and angry

29

The Earl of Strafford

delegation from Ireland came to testify against him, ensuring his execution. His death was not enough to pacify Ireland's Catholic landowners. To them the English parliamentarians and their Puritan followers, who threatened to topple royal authority, looked a worse prospect than even Charles and Strafford.

A ramshackle alliance of the few remaining native Irish landowners and the Old English sparked a nationwide insurrection in 1641. All the bitterness that had been fermenting for years quickly turned into a craving for revenge. Thousands of Protestants were killed, and many thousands more turned out of their homes, stripped of their clothes and possessions. A year later the Civil War across the sea should have provided the Irish with the perfect opportunity to finish off the remaining British settlers. Instead cracks started appearing in the makeshift friendship between the Catholics. A complex mass of different allegiances, aims and factions bubbled to the surface, virtually paralysing the insurrection.

When Charles was beheaded in 1649 Ireland was still in chaos. The victorious Oliver

Cromwell arrived with twenty thousand troops to stamp order on the island, and avenge the Protestant deaths. His army was the most fit and efficient in Europe, and he was an expert soldier with an iron constitution. The opposition was crushed ruthlessly, often with great cruelty, as Cromwell zealously carried out what he thought was God's will. At Drogheda he massacred thousands after securing victory. Civilians were killed even in the sanctuary of St Peter's Church. A few wretched survivors were deported to the West Indies and sold into slavery. In Wexford his troops went berserk slaughtering two thousand in the marketplace during a parley. Churches were ransacked, priests chased down, books burnt and holy pictures torched.

It was a devastating and costly campaign. In 1653 the English parliament confiscated all land in Ireland to help pay its debts. The poor soils west of the Shannon were destined for the Catholics who could prove they had no connection with the rebels; the rest were executed, exiled, transported, or fined depending on their level of involvement. Land

and power had been redistributed and a new order was in place. English and Scottish Protestants were now the land-owning masters of a Catholic and Gaelic-speaking peasantry.

Even so, the Catholics saw a chance for retribution with the accession of James II, a converted Catholic, in 1685. Anxiety spread through Protestant Ireland after he appointed the Catholic Robert Talbot, Earl of Tyrconnell, as the country's Lord-Lieutenant. Talbot proceeded to raise a large Catholic army. This greatly unnerved the English and the general disquiet forced James to flee to France. His daughter, Mary, and son-in-law, William, both Protestants, seized the throne.

Meanwhile the new Catholic parliament in Ireland passed an Act to confiscate all Protestant property, reversing Cromwell's legacy. James landed in Ireland backed by French forces, though crucially this time without the support of the Pope, who had had a quarrel with France. Except for the Protestant strongholds of Derry and Enniskillen, the Catholics at last had control over the whole country, and a Catholic king to lead them. James tried to take Derry, putting it under siege for fifteen weeks. The town so nearly fell, before the English fleet sailed in to relieve it. In 1690, King William landed in Ireland with 36,000 men, and in July, he defeated James at the Battle of the Boyne. James, whose heart was never really in it, once again fled to France. The Catholics went on fighting and before their final defeat a year later, William promised them freedom of worship, protection from persecution and the restoration of their estates.

Instead, the early eighteenth century saw the passing of stringent Penal Laws. Catholics were forbidden from parliament, the bench and the bar, from voting and bearing arms, from university and all public institutions. Their land passed into Protestant hands, and Catholic families were torn apart by laws allowing new Protestant converts to claim their fathers'

The law courts in eighteenth-century Dublin

estates. Bishops were banished and faced being hung, drawn and quartered if they came back. A system of total oppression had been put in place; Catholics made up three-quarters of the population, but they owned only a tiny portion of the land and had been excluded from all positions of power.

(*Overleaf*) The Battle of the Boyne *by Jan Wyck*

ascendancy and emancipation

During the eighteenth century, the brutality of the Penal Laws became increasingly unpalatable to the educated and enlightened section of Protestant Ireland. To them, existing laws such as the Woollen Act and Cattle Act, which strangled the development of Irish enterprise, were proof that the English parliament did not have the country's best interests at heart. A new sense of Irishness was born that operated above the religious divide to bring both Catholic and Protestant Irish together against the English.

By the 1760s, this emerging idea of nationhood manifested itself in a small but influential following in the Irish parliament, the 'patriots' led by Henry Grattan. They called for Irish legislative independence under the crown. When regular troops were deployed to fight in the American War of Independence, the patriots had an excuse to raise an army, the Irish Volunteers, ostensibly to

Parliament Square, Trinity College, Dublin

keep order and guard against invasion. In effect, the Volunteers mobilized public opinion and were instrumental in winning greater commercial freedom, relief for Catholics and apparent legislative independence in the so-called 'Grattan's parliament' of 1782–1800.

(Overleaf) The Volunteers on College Green
by Francis Wheatley

More radical voices such as those of Theobald Wolfe Tone and his United Irishmen were demanding total separation from England and a union between Irish of all religions. As revolution gripped France, ideas spread of a similar Irish republic. By 1798, Tone's society had 280,000 members and in the summer rebellion erupted across the country. Lack of co-ordination, resources and strategy put a quick end to the insurrections. Tone himself was captured in a French warship off the coast and condemned to death, but committed suicide first. Contrary to Tone's wishes, passions spilled over into sectarian violence in some areas. At Wexford, two hundred Protestant prisoners were burnt to death in a barn.

To the English it was clear that neither Grattan's parliament nor the great landowners of the Protestant Ascendancy had the capacity to keep Irish affairs under control. William Pitt, the Prime Minister, saw union between the two islands as the best solution. Catholics supported union, having been told that emancipation would soon follow. On 1 January 1801 the

United Kingdom of Great Britain and Ireland came into being. The emancipation of the Catholics, on the other hand, did not. Pitt had buckled under George III's opposition to it.

It took a man of great dynamism to rally the dispirited Catholic masses and to form an organized political voice for them. Daniel O'Connell, a skilled orator and master of political dramatics, drummed up a nationwide body of support for his Catholic Association, facilitated in part by the 'Catholic rent', a membership fee of a penny a month. By 1828 his following was so great that he was elected MP for Clare, but as a Catholic was forbidden to take his seat at Westminster. A year later, parliament reversed this, giving Catholics the right to hold public office – an important victory.

During the next quarter of a century, O'Connell strove to repeal the Union. He joined with the 'Young Irelanders', who had a more militant attitude. 'Monster meetings' were

Daniel O'Connell

organized for the combined following, and it was during one of these at Clontarf in 1843 that O'Connell was arrested for seditious conspiracy and imprisoned. He was released a month later, but was a shadow of his former self. The Young Irelanders went on to insurrection in 1848. It was a shambles, ending up as a scuffle in 'Widow McCormack's cabbage patch' and the leaders were deported to Tasmania. In any case, at that time Ireland was in no state to revolt. Politics mattered far less than survival in a country so ravaged by hunger and death.

Conditions could not have been more conducive to a major disaster. Ireland was suffering from desperate poverty. Over half of rural families lived in windowless mud cabins, perhaps a dozen people crammed into a single room with animals and mess all about. In addition, the population was soaring and being forced to live off increasingly small subdivisions of land. In fact, it was the most densely populated country in Europe. The only food that could support large numbers of people on such pitiful fragments of land was the potato, and Ireland's rural poor were completely dependent on it. The average family ate five tons of potatoes a year.

In the summer of 1845, a mysterious blight turned over half the country's potatoes into inedible, putrefying sludge. In 1846, blight struck again, destroying almost the entire crop. This calamity was followed by one of the country's worst ever winters. The next year's crop was largely spared: unfortunately the extent of famine was so bad by then that most seeds had been eaten and very few planted. For many thousands there was simply no food. It is hard to imagine the scale of distress, disease and death that Ireland underwent in those years. Many who escaped starvation were overcome by typhus, dropsy and cholera in the squalor of the workhouses. Others fled the land for America,

*A family leaves their one-roomed cottage in Cork to join relatives
who had settled in America in 1832.*

packing the notorious 'coffin ships' often unfit for passage and rife with disease. Thousands survived the journey only to die in the overcrowded, pestilent quarantine stations in the New World.

A million people perished in the great famine of 1845–50, and another million and a half emigrated to America. Ireland had lost a fifth of its population and was never the same again. The British government was blamed for not doing nearly enough to lessen the tragedy, for blindly following the hard-line *laissez-faire* policies of the day. For the Irish in America, the horror of the famine and the heartlessness of the British were realities frozen in time. The increasingly powerful Irish Americans would go on to provide money and support to a range of republican movements, to the Fenians immediately after the famine, and to the many others of future years.

struggle and resolution

In the second half of the nineteenth century, the nationalist mood intensified. The Land League, lead by the MP, Charles Stewart Parnell, a Protestant landowner and a staunch nationalist, managed to secure the Land Act of 1881. The Act reduced rents, ending years of rural violence, eviction and resistance between tenants and landlords, and setting in motion a social revolution, which by 1917 saw two-thirds of Irish farmers take possession of their farms. In 1886, Parnell was also within a whisker of securing success for Home Rule, which promised Irish autonomy within the British Empire, through an alliance with the Liberal Prime Minister, William Gladstone. By 1890, renewed campaigning seemed to put Home Rule back in his grasp, but disaster struck. Parnell was named as co-respondent with Kitty O'Shea in a divorce case. His stunned party imploded beneath him,

Charles Stewart Parnell

and he died the following year aged only 45 having fought in vain to regain his leadership.

Parnell's death dealt a severe blow to the Home Rule movement and the nationalist cause. But while nationalism foundered politically, a new channel for its expression was coming to the fore. Many societies were founded at the end of the century, to stem the erosion of Irish culture and identity. The Gaelic Athletic Association sought to promote traditional Irish games, such as hurling and Gaelic football, threatened by extinction from the spread of English sport. The Gaelic League fought for 'the de-anglicization of Ireland' through the renaissance of the Irish language. In time they won the legal recognition of the language in education. W.B. Yeats and Lady Gregory founded the National Literary Society and the Abbey Theatre, taking inspiration from Irish mythology and history to rekindle Ireland's literary tradition. This surge of interest in Irish culture, the Celtic Revival, gave the people a new confidence in their identity, an important distinctiveness which also justified Irish independence from Britain.

By 1913, the mood had changed and it

Lady Lavery as Cathleen Ni Houlihan *by Sir John Lavery*

looked as though Home Rule could not fail. But to the Ulster Unionists, Home Rule 'meant Rome Rule'. They feared that the industrialized north-east, so dependent on the British Empire, would fall foul of a new Irish parliament. The Ulster Volunteer Force was set up and quickly recruited 100,000 men. Shortly afterwards, the Irish Volunteers were formed in the south to counter them. Just when a full-scale civil war looked inevitable, World War I broke out.

Most men on both sides agreed to join the British Army and fight in Europe. A hard core group of Volunteers under the Irish Republican Brotherhood, on the other hand, planned revolution. On Easter Sunday 1916, around two thousand men seized public buildings in Dublin and declared Ireland a republic. Confusion, lack of support from the Germans, and the arrival of overwhelming British forces brought a speedy end to the Easter Rising; the leaders were executed and hundreds more imprisoned.

The majority of the Irish public had been shocked and puzzled at the Rising. After all, many had relatives fighting in the British Army

in Europe. The heavy-handedness of the British response to it, however, quickly swung opinion in favour of the rebels. The public rallied behind Sinn Féin, up till then a fringe organization, but swiftly becoming the open political party of republicanism. Sinn Féin dominated the post-war elections outside the Protestant north-east. The party won 73 seats out of 105, and instead of taking them in Westminster, set up its own Irish parliament, the Dáil Éireann. Eamon de Valera, who was still in prison for his part in the Rising, was elected leader. Shortly after the parliament's first meeting in January 1919, Ireland and Britain slid into an ugly guerrilla war for two-and-a-half years.

The Anglo-Irish treaty of 1921 promised the best chance for peace. It was signed by a delegation led by Michael Collins that December. Although it involved an oath of allegiance to the British Crown and partition between the six counties of the north-east and the other twenty-six, he strongly believed the treaty offered a

(Opposite) The Easter Rising as depicted in Irish Life

'stepping-stone' to a full republic. On his return, it was clear that a sizeable portion of the Dáil did not share his optimism. Differences of opinion soon escalated into civil war between pro- and anti-treaty republicans; Collins himself was a casualty of the fighting. After a year, the pro-treaty forces of the new Irish Free State prevailed.

In the thirties and forties Fianna Fáil, led by de Valera, was the dominant party in politics of the twenty-six counties. De Valera whittled down the State's connections to Britain under the treaty arrangement, and in his constitution of 1937 named the country Éire, defining its territory as the 'whole island of Ireland'. He adopted a course of neutrality throughout World War II. In 1948, the opposition party Fine Gael came to power and finally took the country out of the Commonwealth, so inaugurating the Republic of Ireland. Some talked about the end of partition at this point; the passing of the Ireland Act in Westminster in 1949, however, ensured there would be no such thing without the consent of the Northern Ireland parliament.

In the 1960s, the substantial Catholic minority

Michael Collins killed by terrorists

of Northern Ireland became increasingly vociferous about their civil rights and discrimination at the hands of the Protestant majority. The government was not able to bring in reforms, and a militant Protestant backlash was aroused. Before long, demonstrations were erupting into riots and sectarian fighting. The British Army was called in during 1969, and a year later the provisional Irish Republican Army began targeting the security forces and centres of commerce. In 1972, direct rule of Northern Ireland was imposed from Westminster, and Protestant paramilitaries, such as the Ulster Defence Association and Ulster Volunteer Force, entered the conflict. A quarter of a century of division, hatred, terror and bitter sectarian violence was Northern Ireland's sad fate.

Finally, in the last month of the twentieth century, a flicker of hope shone on Northern Ireland. A fragile peace process, stumbling between ceasefires from stalemate to deadlock, succeeded in bringing about a chance for a lasting solution. A devolved Northern Ireland cabinet at last convened, in which nationalists and unionists sat side by side, working together to lift the shroud of fear and violence that has darkened the island for so many years.